Places, Spaces

Carolia Rain

Places, Spaces

A small book for inspiration

© 2023 Carolia Rain
Cover art & design: Carolia Rain
Layout: Carolia Rain
Publisher: BoD – Books on Demand, Helsinki, Finland
Printed by: BoD – Books on Demand, Norderstedt, Germany

ISBN: 978-952-31-8571-5

It all began with a block in need of breaking. An artist with no new ideas, for there were no new sources of inspiration around.

And another artist, who had too many images floating around in her head to ever paint them all. It seemed like a perfect way to inspire another while also getting those images in good use, to write them out in a form that would hopefully be easily approachable. I took the road of atmosphere and vague details, of feel and colour, for writing in great detail would have just told the reader what the view was, not given their imagination a chance to explore the possibilities.

Then the poems kept coming and soon I had a pile, and I thought that maybe there were others, who would like to read them and see what their imagination comes up with vague prompts, or would just enjoy fragments of places unknown.

And now, dear reader, here we are. Whether you seek for artistic inspiration or a just small moments of poetry about strange places and spaces, I hope you enjoy.

Among the old, old trees
the scent of rain
still lingers – for just a moment more.
And the road?
A rippling mirror
of sunset gold.

Nowhere else
would I feel like a mere speck of dust,
yet a giant,
except here,
where tiny cabins,
humbly grow from the ground,
bowing
their mossy roofs to the mountains
high above.

Early spring sun bears witness
as the fierce roiling joy of a river
– freed
from the shackles of winter,
joined
by the melting snow –
sings and bubbles on its way
through the corner of a forest,
washing away the last reminders
of snow.

A forest of brackens is
slowly taking over
the shady corner of a yard.
And in its cover
happen things
not for the human eyes to see.

Something chimes,
like silvery laugh,
among the whispery sway of leaves.
”Just the last of this morning’s dew.”

I stomp footprints in the blood coloured sand
to prove myself
the view in front of me is not
just an illusion.
The dark grey cliffs
rise from the endless red
like talons
grasping for prey.

Thousands of fallen petals
disappear
in the white waters flowing over a dam.
It is a tiny thing,
unnoticeable really,
in a landscape governed by
a wooden bridge.

From within the mist
a town looms in front,
shadows that,
with thousand bright eyes
of street lamps,
follow your path
through fading sunset.

Their trunks like enormous reeds,
trees lean over a path
bowing
under the weight of snow.

Fence
woven of twigs and grass
groans under its burden.

From mist of a white night
islands appear.
Hundreds of circles
of flowers and grass,
of moss and trees.
Floating past they reunite,
one mass
under the light of the pale moon.

Mid autumn sunset
paints the town with copper.
Slowly
mist spreads to cover the valley
and the centuries
witnessed by the walls
whisper their stories
from the shadowy corners.

As if to contrast
the bright colours of the paper lanterns,
weathered signs
and delicate vines
embrace
the houses
of leisurely meandering street.
Corners of roofs
reach for each other
with absent thoughtfulness.

Cliffs seem black
where the white waves break
roaring
and where the green of grassland
ends
like it has been cut with a knife.

A tree
in the middle of ocean.
Enthusiastically it reaches
for the sun,
fluffs up its needles.

And the ocean sways in the wind,
waves of scent,
made of millions of blue flowers
that mirror the sky.

In the shade of ancient trees
an angel weeps
on her pedestal.
Around her
rows upon rows
of mossy stones.

From holes of a tree stump,
beneath polypores,
from among mosses
and beyond small bridges
tiny lights glimmer.

And a being, old and branch like
nods, content.
The purl of a stream echoes
into the falling night.

Built from shipwrecks,
it was,
a pirate's harbour.
Bright coloured town
of endless paths
and bridges
connecting houses.

Gnarled trees sway above ,
raining
their purple flowers
on travellers hair.
The road is crowned by scent and shadows.

Waterfall after waterfall
the river travels,
down,
down.
Stone bridge hidden in the cliffside,
covered
with centuries of moss.

An island
in the middle of a lake.
Like a patchwork canvas,
it expands.

Over the centuries a manor
built its own royal court
of houses and storerooms,
balancing at the very edge of water.

A wooden bridge
crossing a wintry river,
like painted by Monet.
But the moment is calmer.
Cleaner.

Cracks of the scorched clay
have come to life,
and now
to the boundlessness
the desert blooms in yellows
and in purples.
Like countless riverbeds,
the flowers flow across plain
and between
wind beaten mesas.

River rapids rushing
between green cliffs
and black rocks,
weaving,
running to distant plains.
There it splits,
divides.
Settles.

Just a few storefronts
add colour
to the grey day in the city.
And rain – picking up again –
begins yet another day
of sharp scented symphony.

Still waters
line the crumbling ruins
withholding secrets,
thousands of them.
Only mirror of a lake,
ancient stones,
and wide clear sky.

It has been decades
since this library closed.
Now
curtain of ivy
embraces the stories of centuries,
bathing in the sunlight
filtering through the roof.

The snow globe sky is grey,
air stands still
when once again
trees
wrap them selves in white.
Dancing
like paw prints made of snow
huge flakes float down,
down,
disappear.

Once again the leaves dance
To the beat of erratic wind.
The autumn forest swirls
In orange, red, and gold.

Wind
carries the scent of freedom
as a row boat
peeks
through the reeds.
Between the gathering clouds
and glittering water
the screams of a seagull echo.

The stairs go down,
down down,
past the last
flickering light.
I stand here and pretend
I can convince myself
that all I hear
is dripping water,
echoes,
the wind,
and it all comes
from the darkness
below.

Winter browned leaves
and yellow grass
welcome the spring with flowers
in melted spots of snow.

The waterline rocks greet
the roaring sea
that crashes toward heavens
as a white foam.
Plants of the barren shore
dig in to stones,
cliffside,
sand,
when the storm rises.

Last night
Autumn
bled trees bright red,
and on the grass
glitter a million needles of ice.

A pathway,
overgrown,
twisting,
after the old locked gate
travels its winding path
around the wilderness
of former flower beds.

Like grasping claws
branches
reach over the path.
Sunlight still sneaks past them
to dance on the forest floor.

The house, once so mighty
is now an enclave of ferns,
that climb its walls
digging their roots
between the tilework.
Flourishing
like no-one else there ever did.

From the fluff of mosses
tiny white mushrooms rise
like straight from a storybook.
They sun themselves
on the trunk of a fallen tree
in the middle
of the colour show of fall.

In the middle of the fields
there is a line.
A line
that not a single sprig of lavender
nor a rebellious oat
dares to cross.
Yet they lean towards each other
like yearning.

Something
brushes against the reeds
and reaches the water.
For a moment
the chime of droplets
joins
the midnight choir
of early summer.

Flags fly proud
above the celebration,
a carnival across the town.
I can hear the sound,
even through the windows
it echoes
in these abandoned halls.

Sunflowers look
as a new day rises
from the rays of gold
shining brightly
among the last shreds of storm clouds.

In the moonlight
white irises
glow in the night black garden
silver on their petals,
crystal pearls on their leaves.

It is hard to say
whether the grey-green-motley-globe
that slowly turns at the end
of a too pale stem
is an alien creature,
or just one more weird mushroom.

Sunlight begins to fade,
not through time
but distance.
Water all around me,
this reverse aquarium.
Oh, I've seen such wondrous things.
Oh, how the structure groans.

Once
there used to be a railroad
passing through here.
It left behind a brick tunnel
and steep encampments,
a monument of days gone by.
Now they frame the sea of flowers blooming
where the rails once lay.

Boats
glide on the river
like in a snow storm.
Cherry blossoms rain
from the ancient trees
reaching over the water.

Old, old maple trees
glow in their autumn dress,
their gnarled branches
so bright in the sunlight
that reaches the kitchen table.

Chalk white wall
peeks out around windows.
Otherwise the house
has wrapped itself in a curtain
of sprawling vines,
a blanket of blossoms,
blue and fragrant.

Brand new asphalt
has bent and cracked,
old roots too stubborn to move.
And from a crack,
new growth of a rowan tree
is sprouting through.

Shelf after shelf
bending under the weight of
dusty scrolls
and tomes.
A lone ray of sun
breaks the forever darkness
and in the long forgotten hall
the dust particles dance.

Ancient houses
reach their floors above the river.
The lanterns hanging from edges of
decorated roofs
shine their light
on the watery highways of the town.

Like sharp edged, stony mushroom
a city grows from a cliffside.
It has been there for centuries,
the change of eras visible
in its walls.

A day of greyest fog
transforms a gothic town
from a historical curiosity
into a stage of a horror tale.
Bright colours of souvenir store
a bridge back to reality.

A street winds down the hill
between houses,
closely build and cheery.
Ivy
curls upon weathered decorations
on the walls.
And street, it changes from cobble
to sand
to stones
to mosaic
and back,
between one building and the next.

A bridge
crosses a river of green and blue.
It has been maintained,
fixed and expanded,
covered.
Over the years
a house grew upon it.

Enormous trunk of a time worn tree
is draped by moss, lichen, woven roads.
The path build upon bog
and backwater
continues up,
up high,
to the village hiding in treetops.

City of arches
carved from the whitest marble
stands as an island
in the middle of the sea.
Like a sophisticated oasis,
it welcomes a traveller.

Between the waterfalls
a castle
casts its magnificence
against the sky.
In its silhouette the windows glitter,
competing
with the moon and stars.
So bright its lights
that shine
upon the dim,
grim and muddy
village
bowing low below,
far from its grace.

Twisted trees sway
and reach,
as shadows creep further,
as light fades
from gold to copper.

Uniform, well planned chaos
of tile-red roofs
spreads out
around the bell tower.
Only a glimpse here,
another there,
of bright coloured walls
break the monotony of the view.

The road opens up
all the way
from here to horizon,
across the sea of flowers,
past over grown ruins,
and through a patch of trees.
On top of this hill
the wind dances,
and I feel like a bird.

Cold grey of rain
paints the neon colours brighter,
a highlighter
of city never quieting.

Scent of dust
on my skin
as I sit down,
rest a while.
The wind picks up,
offering no comfort.
It carries only
the heat of asphalt,
of sun baked empty streets.

Moor
like a bright green ocean
swells and surges
from here
to where
a grand forest of ancient trees
looks insignificant and small,
and then it continues on.

Spring morning sun
glitters between young birches
while mist and breeze
dance their golden dance
between sleeping horses.

From the walls of fog
the trees crane
their gnarly branches towards
the winding
narrow path
like hungry ghosts.

Centuries, never ceasing,
the wind
has torn at the trees on the coast.
Now they grow crooked,
bent to the shape the wind wills them.
But they grow.

At the corner of stone steps,
a small batch of growth hides in.
Sea anemones
wave their tentacles
reaching out
in the safety
of a sunken ruin.

Glossy red apples
sway slowly,
stretching their stems.
They are planning to aim
at the moss
of the bonsai pot.

Above the river,
a path has been woven.
Beneath the blossoms
a small boat adrift.

Rain.
On lily pads,
then
chiming straight past them.
Light coloured flowers
covered in pearls of rain
just for a moment,
and then – again!

The trunks are alive.
Thousands of tiny mushrooms
reaching their striped caps
toward the scattered light.

The filigree on the white shelves
has been hand gilded,
bright,
golden.
Chandeliers and lacy railings
glitter like sky of thousand stars,
crystals
polished to perfection.
The millions of pages on the shelves,
the greatest treasure.

The forest has gone still,
the silence heavy,
waiting.
Among the shadows
something creeps.

Worn window
has dispersed sun rays
into rainbow.
Dried plants,
bottles and jars
on dusty shelves of a murky room
witness the dance of dust.

The night traffic
echoes from distance.
The flashes of light
warped by the rain
that washes away
the stains of day.

Ruins of ancient temples
like large hives
keep on gathering
layers upon
layers
of moss
in the middle of moor
that's slowly
turning in to a forest.

Enormous gate
stands like an insignificant ant
in front of a
castle it's supposed to guard.
Like gothic cathedral with dozens of towers and
countless floors
it stands against the inky clouds.
A storm is rising.

Delicate,
sharp spires of the shining city
stand in defiance
of the water
flowing everywhere around them.
It is a losing battle
against a stream that
slowly
eats away roads and squares,
the edges of city,
the memory of people.

Black iron fence
draws a line in the carpet
of red leaves,
between the walkways
and the front yards.
Old street lamps offer their guidance
through
the sea of Autumn.

Paper lanterns
cast their light over
the river edge town.
A small boat
fastened to the front steps,
under the cover of upper floors.

I gaze
at the town below,
for centuries sheltered by mountains.
Quietly,
without hurry
it grew
into a patchwork quilt
of all it's eras.

A lone tree
stands guard above a valley.
Beneath,
the cliffsides
turn in to forests,
then meadows,
until a river widens
from rock face to rock face,
and continues on
between the mountains
and further than the eye can see.

Light
filters through the dirty glass
of abandoned green house,
reaching
dusty jars and bottles
on a side table,
overgrown.
Still standing,
a shelf with a sign:
"Pick your poisons."

Thriving willows
circle the reedy pond.
The first frost of a fall
has painted them bright
and dyed
the tips of the reeds.

Only a decrepit wooden fence
knows the line between
the over grown path
and the deceitful tussocks
at the edge of the lake.

Spring verdant mountain side
covered with tiny pools,
like stairs
carved from the blue
of the sky.

Through a forest at nigh
a light shines.
Between snowbanks
reaching its roof
a night train travels,
heading for home.

Early evening gold
paints the landscape
as the children play at the park.
Yellow grass
and red leaves
rustle under the small,
nimble feet.

Lightning
from the ash clouds.
Burning rock
rains
towards the sky,
then back down again.
Fireworks of nature's wrath
colour the nightfall.

Mist wanders among the trees,
dancing from trunk to trunk,
from shadow to shadow,
from shade to light,
in to the ray of setting sun.
And
for a moment,
the forest blazes sun-fire.

In the depth of a primeval vault
never seen fungi
glow a light of their own,
and a layer of fog
wanders between strange statues.

From roof to roof
a pathway
of light bridges
wanders across the town.
And above the houses
and the pergolas on top of them
fly kites,
hundreds of them,
large and bright in sunlight.

Birds have returned
to the winter scorched fields,
and the first green of spring
is creeping
along the riverbank,
like a thief
trying to steal away the lifeless grey.